21st CENTURY LIVES
BRITISH OLYMPIANS

Debbie Foy

WAYLAND

First published in 2009 by Wayland

This edition reprinted by Wayland in 2010

Copyright © Wayland 2009

Wayland
338 Euston Road
London NW1 3BH

Wayland Australia
Level 17/207 Kent Street
Sydney, NSW 2000

Senior editor: Camilla Lloyd
Designer: Simon Borrough
Picture researcher: Diana Morris

Picture Acknowledgments: The author and publisher would like to thank the following for allowing their pictures to be reproduced in this publication: Cover & 9: Bob Thomas/Getty Images; Cate Gillon/Getty Images: 16, David Cannon/Getty Images: 10, Feng Li/Getty Images: 13, Guang Niu/ Getty Images: 12, Jamie McDonald/Getty Images: 18, Jonathan Hordle/Rex Features: 4, Lui Jin/Getty Images: 17, M N Chan/Getty Images: 11, Michael Kappeler/Getty Images: 19, Paul Gilham/Getty Images: 7, Rex Features: 1, 8, 14, 15, 20, 21, Top Group Photo/Rex Features: 6.

British Library Cataloguing in Publication Data:
Foy, Debbie
    British Olympians. - (21st century lives)
    1. Athletes - Great Britain - Biography - Juvenile
    literature 2. Olympics - Juvenile literature
    I. Title
    796'.0922

ISBN: 978 0 7502 5946 0

Printed in China

Wayland is a division of Hachette Children's Books, an Hachette UK company

www.hachette.co.uk

Contents

Rebecca Romero
Going for Gold

On her return from Beijing in summer 2008, Rebecca was a guest at the Nickelodeon Kids' Choice Awards in London.

"I would have been absolutely crushed to have won silver again. To have medals in two different sports – I'm so proud of myself. It's been my goal to be a great athlete, to be a great champion."

Rebecca on her gold medal win, Times Online, 18 August 2008

Full name: Rebecca Jayne Romero

Sport: Track cycling

Date and place of birth: 24 January 1980, Surrey, England

Background: Rebecca grew up in Wallington, Surrey with her mother and sister. Her parents divorced when Rebecca was six years old and money was tight. Rebecca attended Wallington High School for Girls where she participated in many sports. At the age of 17 her family moved house to Twickenham and Rebecca began rowing. Within eight months she was selected for the Junior Rowing World Championships.

Olympic achievements: Rebecca won a silver medal in rowing at the 2004 Olympic Games in Athens. At Beijing 2008 she was awarded with a gold medal in the individual pursuit track cycling event.

You might not know: Along with several other Olympians, Rebecca posed naked on a bicycle in an advertising campaign to promote the sports drink, Powerade, in 2008.

Becoming an Olympian: Rebecca is enormously dedicated to her sport, so much so, that she was despondent when she 'only' won the silver medal in Athens! In Beijing she claimed she would rather die than get another silver medal!

Rebecca on the track in her gold medal-winning women's pursuit race at the Laoshan velodrome.

Rebecca Romero simply doesn't do second best. Her drive and commitment to her sport is bound up coming runner up just does not figure. She is an Olympian in two sports – rowing and cycling – but don't be surprised if she announces she is going for a third ...

At the age of 17 Rebecca decided she would like to take up a water sport. She joined her local club in Kingston and only eight months later, and while still studying for her A-levels, she was selected for the 1998 Junior World Championships. In 2004 Rebecca competed in the Athens Olympics, securing herself a silver medal in the Women's Quadruple Scull rowing event. Disappointed in herself for failing to win the gold, she became disillusioned with rowing and decided to retire.

A cycling coach named Dan Hunt invited her to Manchester velodrome to undergo fitness tests and then offered to train her up for Team GB in the 3-kilometre individual sprint cycling event. Her intense drive to succeed made up for what experience she lacked on a bicycle and though she only had two and half years to train for Beijing she put everything into her training regime. Rebecca's schedule involved cycling five hours a day for six days a week, and when she wasn't cycling she was having sports massages or meeting sports psychologists who helped her to develop a positive mental attitude.

On 17 August 2008 Rebecca Romero sped to gold in the women's 3000m individual pursuit, beating her GB team-mate Wendy Houvenaghel by just two seconds with a win time of 3 minutes 28.321 seconds. As she powered to victory she became the first British woman to win Olympic medals at two separate sports.

For a woman who has wished for victory as much as Rebecca, she finally felt she was living her dream. She is set on another gold medal success at London 2012 and then thinks she might even try a third sport. With her absolute drive and determination she may well succeed, too.

"I've worked with elite female athletes for the last seven years and she is the most driven athlete I have ever met, male or female."

Dan Hunt, Rebecca's coach, Times Online, 18 August 2008

Ben Ainslie
Sailing's Superman

At Beijing 2008 Ben became the most successful British sailor in Olympic history.

"It is between me and the American, which means I just have to stick to him like glue, I just have to make sure I know where he is, get in front if I can and make sure I stay there and then there will be no problems. It is going to be a tough race and whatever lead I have is not enough, especially when the conditions are so fickle."

Ben Ainslie on his competition for the gold medal in Beijing, Times Online, 15 August 2008

Full name: Charles Benedict ('Ben') Ainslie

Sport: Sailing

Date and place of birth: 5 February 1977, Macclesfield, Cheshire

Background: Ben's career in sailing began at the age of eight with his parents and sister in Restronguet, Cornwall. His father Roddy Ainslie had captained a boat that took part in the first Whitbread Round the World Race of 1973-74, so it was a natural progression for young Ben to get into a boat. Ben attended Truro School in Cornwall.

Olympic achievements: 2008 gold medal in the Beijing Olympics (Finn Class); 2004 gold medal at the Athens Olympics (Finn Class); 2000 gold medal at the Sydney Olympics (Laser Class); 1996 silver medal at the Atlanta Olympics (Laser Class).

You might not know: One of Ben's rituals before a big race is to have a Chinese meal!

Becoming an Olympian: Sailing at a high level is very intensive and expensive, so you have to be well organised and funded. However local sailing clubs are relatively cheap and accessible to everyone.

Ben celebrates after winning the gold in the Finn class event in Beijing.

If gold medals are a measure of success then only the rowers Sir Steve Redgrave and Sir Matthew Pinsent stand above Ben Ainslie in their achievements for Great Britain in the Olympic Games. With three gold medals from three consecutive Olympic Games under his belt, people are speculating on whether sailing's 'Superman' will receive a knighthood too. This knighthood would recognise the fact that Ben has dominated Olympic sailing for almost a decade.

Ben began sailing with his family from a young age. His parents were keen sailors and soon Ben's childhood hobby turned into a way of life. By the age of 16 Ben was already Laser Radial World Champion. With the support and enthusiasm of his family Ben went on to win his first Olympic medal at the 1996 Olympic Games in Atlanta, taking the silver in the Laser class.

A gruelling program of training for the next four years paid off at the Sydney Olympics of 2000 where Ben fulfilled every sportsman's ambition of winning a gold medal – again in the Laser class. After a period of a year spent training for the America's Cup, Ben decided to refocus on his Olympic sailing making the transition from the Laser class to the Finn (Heavyweight dinghy)

class. The move to the Finn class meant that Ben had to gain 15 kilos in weight but his efforts were rewarded again when Ben scooped his second gold medal at the 2004 Olympic Games in Athens.

On August 17 2008 the wet and blustery conditions at the Qingdao Olympic Sailing Centre in Beijing were ideal for British sailors and Ben Ainslie dominated the Finn Medal Race to win his third Olympic gold medal. Ben's focus has now switched to the London 2012 Olympics where he will be hoping to add a fourth gold medal to his collection in UK waters. If sailing's 'Superman' can pull off a fourth consecutive gold then Ben Ainslie will really have shown his superhuman powers!

"I thought the Games were a great success. The Chinese couldn't have done more or been more welcoming. It was honour to be a part of such a successful team."

Ben Ainslie interview, www.thefirst90minutes.com, 12 September 2008

Rebecca Adlington
The Golden Girl

Rebecca is a special guest at the Pride of Britain Awards in London, September 2008.

" London 2012, here I come – it's going to be fantastic. I wouldn't miss it for the whole world. "

Rebecca, on her future plans, *The Sunday Times*, 17 August 2008

Full name: Rebecca Adlington

Sport: Freestyle swimming

Date and place of birth: 17 February 1989, Mansfield, Nottinghamshire

Background: Rebecca began swimming at the age of four at the local Sherwood swimming pool. Her competitive edge became evident when trying to keep up with her elder sisters in the pool as the young Rebecca refused to wear arm bands! At the age of six she was identified as having a special talent and at the age of 13 she embarked upon a gruelling training schedule which involved taking a 50-mile round trip in the car, twice a day. Shortly after she was selected for the Nottinghamshire County Swim Squad (Nova Centurion) where she currently trains.

Olympic achievements: In the Beijing Olympics Rebecca won gold medals in the 400m and 800m freestyle events. In December 2008, Rebecca was the second runner-up after Lewis Hamilton at the BBC Sports Personality of the Year award. Chris Hoy won the coveted award.

You might not know: Rebecca would love to be a contestant on her favourite television show, *Strictly Come Dancing*!

Becoming an Olympian: Rebecca's training regime means that she swims between 6am and 8am in the morning, and then between 5pm and 7pm in the evening, six days a week. During the afternoons she usually does an hour or more of running or circuit training.

Rebecca loves designer shoes and her parents promised to buy her a pair by her favourite shoe designer, Jimmy Choo, if she won at the 2008 Olympic Games! Did the promise of designer shoes spur Rebecca Adlington on to swim her way to fame in the 2008 Beijing Olympics? The world watched with awe as the 19-year-old from Mansfield scooped not one but two gold medals in the 400m and 800m freestyle swimming events at the Water Cube in Beijing, setting new British and Olympic records at the same time.

Rebecca began swimming at Sherwood Baths in Mansfield at the age of six, following in the footsteps of her older sisters, Laura and Chloe. She began swimming competitively and was selected for the Nottinghamshire County swimming squad where she currently trains. At the age of 13 Rebecca dedicated herself to a strict training regime and her mother gave up her job as a secretary to ferry her daughter to and from her twice daily training sessions.

EGA

Rebecca celebrates winning the 800m freestyle event in Beijing.

Rebecca's victory on 11 August 2008 in the 400m event was an unexpected thrill. She had been ranked 4th in the world in the heats, but won the event on the final touch with just a 0.07-second margin over the American favourite Katie Hoff. On the 16 August in the 800m event Rebecca led from the start, crushed the opposition and powered to victory to win by more than six seconds.

Her phenomenal success in the Olympics resulted in several accolades: She is the first British woman to win an Olympic swimming gold in nearly half a century (the last was Anita Lonsbrough in 1960). In the 800m event Rebecca also set the world record in distance freestyle swimming with 8 minutes 14.10 seconds, breaking the current world record of 8 minutes 16.22 seconds set by the American Janet Evans.

A victory parade through Mansfield greeted Rebecca on her return to the UK from Beijing and the Mayor of Mansfield presented her with a pair of gold Jimmy Choo high heels! She is looking forward to London 2012 and if her current success is anything to go by she should probably make sure she has enough cupboard space for all those pairs of shoes!

"I'm delighted that the records I held for being the last British woman to win a swimming gold medal are finally gone – and they could not have gone to a more lovely or deserving athelete."

Anita Lonsbrough, Olympic gold medallist swimmer (1960), *The Sunday Times*, 17 August 2008

Lee Pearson
Riding High

Lee Pearson attends an award event in Portugal sporting his patriotic bow tie!

"I've got to do London 2012, to do the Paralympics in your own country is going to be amazing. With the right funding, I could even do the Olympics. You find me a few million to fund me an Olympics horse and I'll ride it in London."

www.universalsports.com,
11 September 2008

Full name: Lee Pearson, MBE (Member of the British Empire), OBE (Order of the British Empire)

Sport: Para-equestrian dressage

Date and place of birth: 4 February 1974, Cheddleton, Staffordshire

Background: Lee grew up in the country with his parents and his two older brothers, Darren and Damien. At the age of six he was given a pet donkey and began riding lessons at eight years old. By the age of 15 Lee had bought his own horse.

Olympic achievements: Lee has achieved an astounding nine gold medals in the last three Olympic Games. He has won three gold medals in the championship dressage, freestyle dressage, and team dressage events at the 2000 Sydney, 2004 Athens and 2008 Beijing Paralympics.

You might not know: Lee's first brush with the media was in 1980 when he was only six years old! Prime Minister Margaret Thatcher carried him up the stairs into 10 Downing Street having awarded him a 'Children of Courage' medal.

Becoming an Olympian: Lee did not discover the possibilities of disabled sport until he saw the 1996 Atlanta Paralympics on television. His positive attitude to his disability has led to his great success. He regards himself as one of the world's luckiest people because he is among the few who have the opportunity to do a job he loves.

Lee Pearson is flash and brash, he enjoys jet-skiing, racing quad bikes and clubbing, but he is also the undisputed world number 1 in his sport with nine Olympic gold medals, an MBE, an OBE and six World Championships to his name. His energy, positivity, drive and enthusiasm make Lee Pearson the perfect embodiment of the Paralympic spirit.

Lee was born with arthrogryposis, a condition in which the muscles in his arms and legs grew deformed in the womb. However, his parents were determined to make his life as normal as possible and though he attended a special needs' school early in his life, from the age of nine he attended mainstream schools.

His brothers loved BMX riding and though Lee wasn't allowed to join them, his parents bought him Sally the donkey to ride on in the paddock of their home. His love of horse riding grew and he took lessons, but it wasn't until he saw the Atlanta Paralympics of 1996 that he realised he might be able to live his dream of working with horses full time. At that point Lee was working in the back room of a supermarket pricing up stock, but he was depressed and desperately wanted to move on.

Horses were his salvation. Lee mastered the art of dressage by wearing plastic splints from his backside to his heels while on horseback. As he has little use of his legs Lee developed a method of controlling the horse by using the strength of his hips, backside and spine. He started competing in para dressage events in 1998 and by 2000 had qualified for the Sydney Olympics in which he scooped the first of his triple golds. In 2003 he became the only disabled person to have won a title at the British Dressage National Championships, competing against able-bodied riders.

Lee currently runs his own stables and trains and competes against able-bodied riders. He is looking forward to adding to his medal haul at the London 2012 Paralympics and has suggested that given the right funding he could even compete at the Olympics. With Lee's success and determination, who knows where we might see him next?

Lee on his horse Gentleman competing in Beijing.

"We are delighted that Lee has been chosen to head the new International Committee. Lee is one of the most successful riders in the world and this choice of Chair reflects the importance that the International Equestrian Federation attaches to Paralympic sport."

Hugh Thomas, Chairman of the British Equestrian Federation (BEF) on Lee Pearson's appointment as Chairman of the Athlete's Committee, www.bef.co.uk, 16th April 2007

Sarah Storey

A Storey of Success

Sarah proudly shows off her medal after winning the women's individual pursuit event at the Laoshan velodrome, 10 September 2008.

> **❝Keep your mind open and suck in the experience, if it hurts – it's probably worth it!❞**
>
> **Sarah Storey's advice on getting to the top,**
> **www.sportingchampions.org.uk**

Full name: Sarah Joanne Storey

Sport: Paralympic cycling

Date and place of birth: 26 October 1977, Manchester

Background: Sarah grew up in Cheshire in a sports-mad family. She began swimming at the age of four and swam for a local club, the Disley Dolphins. At High School Sarah competed in all able-bodied sports. She represented Cheshire in cross-country running and netball and was also the Cheshire County Champion in table tennis for three consecutive years. She studied for a degree in Sports Science while continuing with her swimming training.

Olympic achievements: Barcelona (1992): Gold medals in 100m backstroke, 200m individual medley. Silver medals in 400m freestyle, 4 × 100m freestyle, 4 × 100m medley team. Bronze medal in 100m freestyle. Atlanta (1996): Gold medals in 200m individual medley, 100m breastroke, 100m backstroke. Silver medal in 400m freestyle. Bronze medal in 100m freestyle. Sydney (2000): Silver medals in 100m backstroke, 4 × 100m medley team. Athens (2004): Silver medals in 100m breastroke, 200m individual medley. Bronze medal in 100m freestyle. Beijing (2008): Gold medals in Women's individual time trial, Women's individual pursuit.

You might not know: When Sarah was competing in the Barcelona Paralympics as a 14-year-old, Blue Peter came along to watch and interview her!

Becoming an Olympian: Her days are varied either by doing track sessions in the velodrome or road training for anything from three to six hours. She often rides between 80 and 120km per day. She also does stretching and core strength work a few times each week. If she has a weekend competition she will take Thursday as her day off to rest and gather her energy.

Sarah Storey, the cycling star of the Beijing Paralympics is unique for many reasons. She has already hit the heights of success in another sport and is the proud record-holder of the most medals won by a female paralympian swimmer in Great Britain. However, in 2005 Sarah swapped the pool for the velodrome and has since won another raft of medals in cycling!

Another gold medal success for Sarah in the women's time trial event in Beijing.

Sarah Storey was born with a deformed hand in which the bones had failed to develop properly, but she has never let it get in the way of her love of sport.
She began swimming at the age of four and a couple of years later while watching the 1984 Olympic Games held in Los Angeles, California, the young Sarah made a pact with herself that she was going to be an Olympian.

She joined a swimming club in Stockport, Manchester and at the age of 14 competed in her first Paralympics in Barcelona in 1992. In her debut she won the 100 metres backstroke, breaking the world record by nearly four seconds in the process.

Sarah followed up Barcelona with successful appearances at the Paralympic Games in Atlanta, Sydney and Athens - adding to her medal collection with a staggering ten medals over the three Games. In 1998 Sarah was honoured to receive an MBE (Member of the British Empire) from the Queen for her services to sport.

In 2005, after a series of ear infections, Sarah decided to shift her focus from swimming to cycling. At the European Cycling Championships in August 2005, Sarah's first appearance as a top level cyclist, she swept the board with a fantastic five gold medals. Beijing 2008 was Sarah's fifth Paralympic Games, but this time she was competing as a cyclist.

In the Laoshan velodrome in Beijing Sarah celebrated two Olympic gold victories in the individual time trial and individual pursuit, setting a world record in the latter event. To add to her phenomenal swimming success Sarah Storey had become the top disabled female cyclist in the world. Sarah is determined to make London 2012 but will it be paddle power or pedal power that takes her there?

"I can't quite believe I've gone 3:36. That would have got me a top eight place at the main Olympics. The fact that a paralympian can finish in that sort of time and that sort of position is amazing."

Sarah Storey on her world-record breaking time in the individual cycling pursuit in Beijing. www.mirror.co.uk, 11 September 2008

Chris Hoy
The Real McHoy

Chris Hoy and his gold medals arrive back at Heathrow Airport on 25 August 2008.

" Whenever there's a wobble in our team people stop and you can see all the heads look at Chris. Like a pack of wolves, when something spooks all the wolves, they all stop and turn and look at the leader. That's Chris Hoy. "

David Brailsford, British Cycling Performance Director, www.timesonline.co.uk, 20 August 2008

Full name: Christopher Hoy, MBE (Member of the British Empire)

Sport: Track cycling

Date and place of birth: 23 March 1976, Edinburgh

Background: Chris attended George Watson's College, an independent school in Edinburgh. Between the ages of 7 and 14 years, Chris competed in BMX racing competitions, ranking ninth in the world. He began a degree course in physics at St Andrew's University in 1996 but transferred to the University of Edinburgh to be closer to the Edinburgh velodrome where he was training. He graduated with a degree in sports science in 1999.

Olympic achievements: In the 2004 Athens Olympics, Chris was awarded a gold medal for the 'kilo' or 1km time trial race. In the Beijing Olympics he scooped three gold medals for the men's keirin, the men's team sprint and the men's individual sprint. Chris won the prestigious BBC Sports Personality of the Year award in December 2008. He was nominated by phone votes by the public ahead of Lewis Hamilton and Rebecca Adlington.

You might not know: As a schoolboy Chris rowed for Scotland and won a British Championship silver in the Junior Coxless Pairs.

Becoming an Olympian: Chris uses psychology to help him on the track. In the run-up to a race Chris will not allow negative thoughts about losing to enter his head. He tries to 'visualise' the race and see himself winning it.

Chris Hoy, Jamie Staff and Jason Kenny winning the gold medal for Great Britain in the men's team sprint.

At the age of 13 Chris Hoy wrote in his diary that he would like to win an Olympic gold. By the end of the Beijing Olympic Games in August 2008 he had fulfilled this dream four times over! In addition to his Athens 2004 gold medal for the 'kilo' race, Chris achieved superstar status in Beijing with his gold treble in three sprint track cycling events at the Laoshan velodrome.

Chris's cycling career had an unusual start. At the age of six he was so enchanted by the BMX bikes ridden by the children in Steven Spielberg's alien film, E.T. that he pestered his mother to buy him one. She purchased his first bike for £5 from a jumble sale but Chris broke it within two weeks by doing so many wheelies!

He began competitive BMX cycling at the age of seven and by the age of 14 he was ranked in the world's top 10. While still a teenager Chris switched loyalties from BMX racing to other cycling and in 1994 he joined the City of Edinburgh Racing Club where he raced time trials, mountain bike, road and track before concentrating on track sprint cycling. He has also been a member of the Great Britain National Cycling Squad since 1996.

After his championship gold in the 'kilo' event in Athens he was awarded an MBE (Member of the British Empire) to feature alongside his collection of other achievements including two Commonwealth Games gold medals and a medal placing in every World Championship since 1999. In short, over the last ten years Chris Hoy has had an incredible success rate.

When Chris discovered in late 2005 that his favourite 'kilo' event was to be axed from the Beijing games to make way for BMX as a medal event, he was forced to change strategy and learn new disciplines within his sport. So, in order to compete in Beijing he had to put all his energies into learning the keirin event. He needn't have worried; such is the strength of Chris's character and motivation that by 2007 he was world champion in the keirin event, too.

Not only is Chris Hoy the first Briton in a hundred years to sweep a triple gold, he is a sporting hero, a true champion and an inspiration to his fans and team-mates.

"If I turned up at a race feeling under-prepared, not having trained as hard as I possibly could, not having looked after my diet, I would be thinking, I wonder if I had done that differently ... I don't want to be in that position standing on the podium in second or third place – or not having made the podium – and thinking 'what if ...'"

Chris Hoy on his psychological preparation for a race, *Scotland on Sunday*, 28 September 2008

Eleanor Simmonds
Teen Swim Sensation

Thirteen-year-old Eleanor proudly displays her two gold medals on her return from Beijing in September 2008.

"In the last 25 metres I just got my head down and went for it. I have dreamed of being a Paralympic medallist but didn't think it would happen yet. I imagined this race in a dream – I finished in the medals but I did not dream I would win the gold, I'm really happy."

Eleanor on her 100m freestyle performance,
www.news.bbc.co.uk/sport,
8 September 2008

Full name: Eleanor Simmonds

Sport: Paralympic swimming

Date and place of birth:
11 November 1994, Walsall, West Midlands

Background: Eleanor began swimming at the age of five at Boldmere Swimming Club in Sutton Coldfield, Birmingham, but in 2007 her family moved to Swansea to be close to the British Swimming High Performance Centre. Eleanor currently attends Olchfa Comprehensive School in Swansea.

Olympic achievements: At the Beijing Olympics Eleanor achieved gold medals in the Women's 100m and Women's 400m freestyle events. Eleanor was named BBC Young Sports Personality of the Year in December 2008.

You might not know: Aside from being an Olympic swimmer, Eleanor would most like to be a forensic scientist.

Becoming an Olympian: Alongside her schoolwork Eleanor puts in nine 2-hour training sessions a week and benefits from the support of her family.

On 7 September, the night before competing in the 100m freestyle event at the Beijing Olympics, Eleanor Simmonds had a dream that she won a silver medal. The day after her dream became a reality – almost – as Eleanor secured not the silver but the gold medal by coming from behind in the last 25 metres to pip Holland's Mirjam de Koning-Peper to the final touch. The girl whom coaches had tipped as being a favourite for a gold in London 2012 had achieved phenomenal success in Beijing. She had become Britain's youngest individual Paralympic gold medallist and her favourite event – the Women's 400m freestyle – was still to come!

Eleanor was born with achondroplasia, or dwarfism, a condition which limits growth. A determined child, Eleanor began swimming at the age of five. As her talent developed her family moved from Birmingham to Swansea so that Eleanor could be close to a 50-metre pool for training. After watching Nyree Lewis win the gold in the 100m backstroke at the Athens Paralympics in 2004 Eleanor was inspired to become a Paralympian.

On 14 September Eleanor made her dream complete, with a second gold medal to add to her previous success, this time in the Women's 400m freestyle.

When she won the event in a world-record time of 5 minutes 41.34 seconds she showed remarkable maturity by announcing that she had another job to do – to offer her support and sympathy to her heroine Nyree Lewis who was devastated after winning only one silver medal from four events.

The teenager received a hero's welcome on her return to the UK. She was chauffeured to school in a limousine to be greeted by hundreds of cheering pupils carrying banners. Most of them had witnessed her victory on a big screen at school. Eleanor Simmonds then received her third gold medal of 2008 – in the form of a giant 'gold medal' cake to celebrate her success!

The moment Eleanor became the champion in the women's 400m final – setting a new world record in the process!

"Eleanor's very dedicated and enthusiastic about the sport. She also has a great support team with mum and dad and she's got a real desire and determination. She doesn't make a big fuss about things but just quietly gets on with the job."

Lars Humer, Head Coach for the GB disability swimming team, www.telegraph.co.uk/sport, 30 April 2008

Tim Brabants
Doctor and Olympian

Tim Brabants combines a career as a doctor with his Olympic success!

> **It's incredible, absolutely incredible. The race went 100 per cent to plan. I need to thank my coach Eric Farrell for 15 years of coaching and now I am Olympic champion. I've had a great season and to finish it up with the most enjoyable race I've ever had is fantastic. Don't be surprised to see me in London ready to represent Great Britain again.**
>
> www.olympics.org.uk/ beijing2008/News, 22 August 2008

Full name: Jules Timothy Brabants

Sport: Flat water canoeing

Date and place of birth: 23 January 1977, Chertsey, Surrey

Background: Tim attended a week-long introductory course at Elmbridge Canoe Club in the school summer holidays of 1987 and has never looked back.

Olympic achievements: Tim was awarded a bronze medal at the 2000 Olympics in Sydney and a gold medal in the 2008 Beijing Olympics, for the 1000m single-man kayak race. He was also presented with the bronze medal at Beijing for the 500m single-man kayak event.

You might not know: Tim has also won a triathlon and likes to go surfing.

Becoming an Olympian: Tim's typical day starts with a session on the water at 7.30am which lasts for around two hours. Following this he usually does a running or swimming session. The afternoon consists of either more paddling on the water or weights in the gym. Around this schedule, there is time built in for recovery, sports massage, physiotherapy and sleep!

...celebrates his gold medal in the 1000m single-man kayak event in Beijing.

his professional career with his sporting interests in a way that is rare among Olympic hopefuls today.

At the Sydney Olympics of 2000 Tim achieved a bronze in the 1000m single-man kayak. But not satisfied with third place, he embarked on a strict training regime to earn himself a place at Athens 2004. When Athens did not see him climbing the podium, Tim returned to his job as a doctor, working in the Accident & Emergency department of a large Jersey hospital.

But fulfilment in sport is like an obsession to Tim and he was always intent on securing a place for himself at the 2008 Beijing Olympics. In the lead up to Beijing Tim worked half the Olympiad (the 4 years in-between each Games) and trained for the second half. On 22 August 2008 he scooped the gold for the single-man kayak event. The bronze medal in the 500m event was an added bonus.

A gold medal-winning victory has not been an easy journey for Tim Brabants. Though lottery funding has helped to support the careers of many Olympic hopefuls, Tim Brabants has largely done it the hard way. But at Beijing – his third Olympics – Tim's hard work finally paid off as he nailed a gold medal, fulfilling a dream that he had been chasing for nearly a decade.

Described by his parents as a 'restless and energetic boy', Tim's mother took him along to a week-long canoe course at their local club in Weybridge, Surrey when Tim was ten years old. Initially he enjoyed simply being on the water, but then he was introduced to racing and began to enter competitions when he was only 12 years old.

Alongside his sporting commitments Tim has trained to be a medical doctor, and since then has combined

Now Tim has achieved his gold, is London 2012 still a big draw? Yes, but first Tim will go back to his job as a doctor. As London 2012 draws near, Tim will likely change from a single boat to a crew, where the expectations and pressures on his body are not so intense. Here's hoping that that the good doctor will add to his medal collection on his home turf ...

"That went even better than I thought it would go. We were expecting gold but just the way he actually raced it from the first stroke he was in front, he just flew out the blocks."

Tim Brabants' coach, Eric Farrell, on his gold medal victory, www.telegraph.co.uk/sport, 22 August 2008

Christine Ohuruogu
Queen of the Track

Christine is a special guest at the GQ magazine awards, September 2008.

❝ People have come out with all these stories about how they stopped work and were screaming at the TV – it's crazy. But I'm really glad I gave you guys a bit of excitement for 10 minutes! ❞

Christine on the reaction to her gold medal-winning sprint, *Sport Magazine*, 17 October 2008

Full name: Christine Ijeoma Ohuruogu

Sport: Athletics

Date and place of birth: 17 May 1984, Newham, East London

Background: Born to Nigerian parents Christine is the second eldest of a family of eight children. She grew up in Stratford, east London and was awarded a linguistics degree from University College London. She played netball for England as a teenager but at the age of 16 she joined the athletics club Newham and Essex Beagles.

Olympic achievements: Christine won the gold medal at Beijing 2008 in the 400 metres sprint event.

You might not know: Christine was raised in Stratford, east London which is less than a mile from the London 2012 Olympic stadium. Her sister, Victoria Ohuruogu, is also a top sprint competitor and is also tipped to be a star in the London Olympics!

Becoming an Olympian: Christine believes that sprinting is not about being the fastest but about having the greatest will and self-belief. She has been taught by her coach to go into every race expecting to win.

...tine celebrates her success for Great ...in in the 400m sprint.

The name 'Ohuruogu' means 'determination' – a quality that Christine seems to have by the bucket load. This determination has seen her become the 400m Commonwealth Champion of 2006, the 400m World Champion of 2007 and in the Beijing Summer Olympics of 2008 she added the honour of Olympic Champion by winning another gold medal in a breathtaking 400m sprint event.

Christine was raised by her hardworking parents, Jonathan and Patience who emigrated to England from Nigeria in the 1980s. She attended a local school and was a hardworking student, achieving ten GCSEs and four A-levels. Through most of her schooling Christine wasn't interested in athletics. The sport she loved was netball; she began playing at the age of nine and represented England at under-17 and under-19 level. She began to win sprint races at school and was persuaded to join her local athletics club. Her potential to be a great sprinter was quickly identified and while studying for her degree Christine kept up a strict training schedule and competed in the European Junior Championships and in the 2004 Athens Olympics.

But in 2006 something happened that put Christine Ohuruogu's determination to the test. All athletes are required to be tested frequently to ensure they are not using drugs to increase or enhance their performance. Christine missed three competition drugs tests in October 2005 and June 2006. She received a one-year ban for missing the tests and the

British Olympic Association banned her from ever competing in future Olympic Games for Great Britain. Christine appealed on the grounds that she was not a cheat and did not take drugs to enhance her abilities, but that she was simply disorganised and had forgotten that the tests were due. On 27 November 2007 Christine won her appeal and her Olympic ban was lifted.

At the Bird's Nest Stadium on 19 August 2008, the bad times behind her, Christine drew on her fierce determination to surge down the track and defeat her rivals. It was the first track medal for Britain and made Ohuruogu the first British female Olympic 400m champion.

Christine's staying power is such that London 2012 must be well within her sights – after all, it is practically on her doorstep!

"The strength told in the end; the strength of mind; the strength of character and the strength of her body."

Steve Cram, BBC commentator and former sprint Olympian, as Christine crossed the finishing line in the 400m sprint, www.dailymail.co.uk/news, 20 August 2008

Other British Olympians

**Bradley Wiggins –
Track and Road Cycling**

Bradley was born on 28 April 1980 in Belgium. His father was a professional cyclist and following in his footsteps Bradley started cycling early on. By 12 he was racing at the Herne Hill velodrome in south London.

Bradley has had considerable Olympic success, winning a bronze medal in his first Olympic appearance at Sydney in 2000 in the team pursuit squad. In the 2004 Athens Olympics Bradley became the first athlete in 40 years to win three medals at a single Olympic Games, winning a gold in the individual pursuit, a silver in the team pursuit and a bronze in the 'Madison' event. At the end of 2004 he was awarded an OBE (Order of the British Empire) for his services to sport.

After participating in the 2006 and 2007 Tours de France he returned to track cycling and in the 2008 Beijing Olympics achieved a further two gold medals in the 4km individual pursuit and the team pursuit. Bradley became the first rider ever to successfully defend his title (earned at Athens 2004) in the individual pursuit. In October 2008 he published his autobiography *In Pursuit of Glory*.

Victoria Pendleton – Cycling

Known as the 'Queen of British track racing', Victoria Pendleton was born on 24 September 1980 in Bedfordshire. She rode her first race at nine and at the age of 13 she was spotted by a national track coach, but chose to pursue a degree in Sport and Exercise Science at Northumbria University before becoming a full time cyclist.

Though she failed to come home with a medal during the Athens Olympics of 2004, she has had at least one major medal win each year in the World Championships or in the Commonwealth Games since then.

In Beijing 2008 all her Olympic hopes were pinned on one event – the Women's sprint. When she crossed the line ahead of Anna Meares in the final of the Women's sprint on 19 August she was overwhelmed that she had won a gold as this had been her dream since 2004. Let's hope London 2012 will see Victoria Pendleton repeating her success!

**Phillips Idowu –
Athletics (Triple Jump)**

Triple jumper Phillips Olaosebikan Idowu was born on 30 December 1978 in Hackney, London. As well as his sporting achievements, Idowu has become known for his flamboyant personality and appearance. He often colours his hair and wears facial piercings and coloured earrings.

Before reaching the age of 20 Phillips Idowu won the English School Championships and ranked fourth place in the European Junior Championships. The Commonwealth Games of 2002 in Manchester saw Phillips win his first major international medal (a silver), followed up by a gold at the Commonwealth Games in Melbourne in 2006.

In March 2008 Idowu won his first world title, scooping the gold at the World Indoor Championships in Valencia, Spain. His 17.75m jump also broke the Commonwealth and British indoor record previously held by triple jumper Jonathan Edwards.

He arrived at his third Olympic Games in Beijing as the favourite to win, but was awarded the silver behind World Champion Nelson

Evora. In interviews Phillips revealed that he was disappointed not to have achieved the gold but was looking forward to London 2012 to achieve his dream!

Danielle Brown – Paralympic Archery

Gold-medal winning paralympic archer Danielle Brown was born on 10 April 1988. A keen runner, Danielle only began to learn archery in 2003 at the age of 16. Within three years she had made it to the international archery squad and became the Junior Indoor Champion in 2004 and 2005 and the National Outdoor Champion in 2005.

Danielle suffers from a condition called RSD – reflex sympathetic dystrophy – which results in constant chronic pain in her feet. She now shoots propped on a stool so the weight is off her feet.

Danielle decided to postpone her studies for a law degree at Leicester University as her time was taken up by her preparation for the Beijing Paralympics 2008.

On 13 September 2008 in the Olympic Green Archery Field, Beijing, Danielle took the gold medal in the Women's Open Individual Compound Final. She was forced to put her feelings aside when she knocked out friend and fellow team GB member Mel Clarke in the semi-finals. She is also tipped to be one of the stars of London 2012 so keep your fingers crossed for Danielle!

James DeGale – Middleweight Boxing

When James Frederick DeGale was born on 3 February 1986 his mother looked at him and said: 'He looks like a boxer.' The London-born lad was to prove her right, but did she ever imagine that her youngest child might be standing on the Olympic rostrum as a boxing gold medal winner?

James was a lively and active child who loved sport and dancing. At school his energy often spilled over into trouble-making, so at the age of ten James's father and grandfather introduced him to the local boxing club in north-west London as a way of channelling his energies. They soon discovered that James had a natural fighting flair.

In March 2006 he competed in the Commonwealth Games in Melbourne. Though he was tipped to win he had to settle for bronze, but this only made him more determined. At Beijing 2008 his middleweight fight with Cuban boxer, Emilio Correa served as the pinnacle to James's career as he won 16-14 on points. Will James go professional like several boxers before him or will he retain his amateur status and defend his title at London 2012?

Heather Frederikson – Paralympic Swimming

Born in Wigan on 30 December 1985 Heather Frederiksen learned to swim at the age of five and began to compete at age nine for the Howe Bridge Aces in Leigh, Lancashire.

Once an up-and-coming freestyle endurance swimmer, in 2004 she won the British 10-kilometre Open Water Championship and the 4.5-kilometer British Grand Prix on the same day! Her future in swimming was bright but at the end of 2004 she suffered a serious accident which left her with limited use of her right arm and leg. The doctors told her she would probably never swim again, but Heather set out to prove them wrong. She joined the City of Salford club and got back in the pool. She had to go back to the beginning and learn how to swim again, but soon began to train with renewed vigour and the aim of winning a medal at the Beijing Paralympics 2008.

Success came on 10 September 2008 when Heather won a gold medal with a world record in the 100m backstroke. She also bagged two silver medals in the 100m and 400m freestyle, and a bronze in the 200m individual medley. Frederiksen is back!

Index